Greeting Cards

Anja van Laar

FORTE PUBLISHERS

Contents

ISBN 90 5877 364 7

This is a publication from
Forte Publishers BV
P.O. Box 1394
3500 BJ Utrecht
The Netherlands

For more information about the creative books available from Forte Uitgevers: www.hobby-party.com

Publisher: Marianne Perlot
Editor: Hanny Vlaar
Photography and digital image editing:
Fotografie Gerhard Witteveen, Apeldoorn, the Netherlands
Cover and inner design:
BADE creatieve communicatie, Baarn, the Netherlands
Translation: TextCase, Groningen, the Netherlands

Preface

Do you also like using lots of pictures of small flowers and other small pictures? I have designed four background stencils and two accompanying stencils with shapes which are ideal for making cards with these little gems. Once you get started, you will quickly realize that you cannot stop. This book will show you that the possibilities are endless. Make sure you don't become addicted! I'm curious to know what you will do with these stencils.

I wish you lots of fun!

Thanks to Marianne Perlot for all her help and the home front for all the typing, coaching and not complaining when the entire table was, once again, covered with my work.

Techniques

1. Embossing

Place the stencil on the good side of the card and secure it in place using non-permanent adhesive tape. Turn them over and place them on a light box. Copy the illuminated shapes using the embossing stylus. If you wish, use Pergasoft (Pergamano) to make the embossing easier. I have also used dark card in this book. Emboss these in the evening, possibly with a brighter light in the light box. If you wish to use a colour which is, in fact, too dark, emboss lines on the card, because these can be embossed according to your own initiative.

2. 3D cutting

First, cut out the entire picture. When cutting out the next layer, look to see what you wish to have in the background and do not cut out these bits. Cut out as many layers as you want in the same way. Most of the pictures in this book are not made from too many layers, because the card becomes too heavy. If you use less pictures, cut the incisions far into the card. Most of the shapes are stuck on the cards using 3D glue and the pictures are stuck on top. You can add as much or little glue as you wish under the pictures, depending on the depth that you wish to create. If you place the glue in a syringe, you have more control over the quantity you apply.

3. Shaping

The flower pictures used in this book are ideal for shaping. Use a shaping mat and a shaping tool, or just use your fingers. With a violet, for example, try to shape the leaves to look like a real violet. When stuck on the card, one leaf may point upwards, whilst the next leaf may point downwards. Since the incisions for the leaves are cut far into the card, they really come alive. The leaves are raised even further by pressing down the middle of the flower when sticking it on the card.

4. Cutting out shapes and cutting along the lines

The shapes on the cards are made using stencils AE 1205 and AE 1206. First, emboss the shape in the card that will be on the top and then cut the shapes out remaining approximately 2 mm from the embossed line. You can also stick the shape on a card of a different colour and cut the shape out leaving a border. This allows you to play with colours.

When cutting along the embossed lines, you must always remain approximately 2 mm from

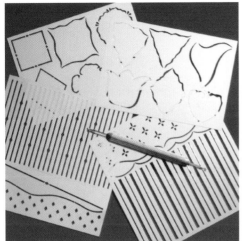

1. The embossing stencils.

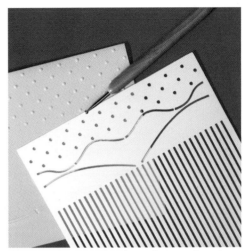

2. Move the stencil and continue embossing.

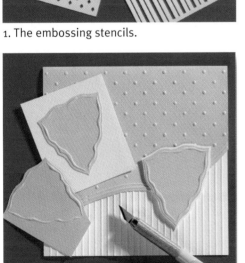

3. Use 3D glue to stick the shapes on the card.

4. Decorate the card with 3D pictures.

the line. Do not throw anything away, because almost everything can be reused. Instead of using a knife, you can also cut the shapes out using a pair of scissors. Do not press to hard when using 3D glue to stick the shapes on the card.

Envelope, size increase 110%

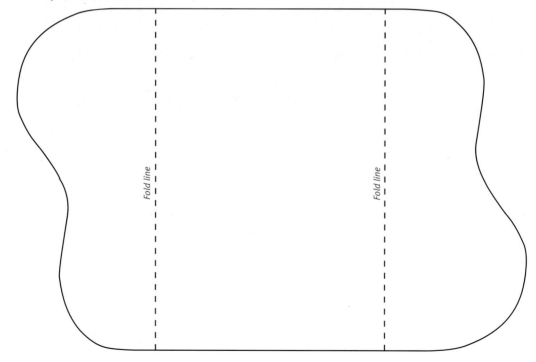

Materials

- Card: Artoz (A), Canson Mi-Teintes (C), Papicolor (P) and coloured embossing paper (K)
- Cutting sheets: Babies 1 and 2, Mini 3D, Shake-it and Janneke Brinkman-Salentijn
- Aslan/double-sided adhesive tape

- Vellum
- Embossing stencils
- Embossing stylus
- Light box
- Gold thread
- Organza ribbon
- 3D scissors
- 3D tweezers

- 3D glue
- Syringe
- 3D shaping pen
- 3D shaping mat
- Cutting ruler (Securit)
- Knife
- Cutting mat
- Photo glue

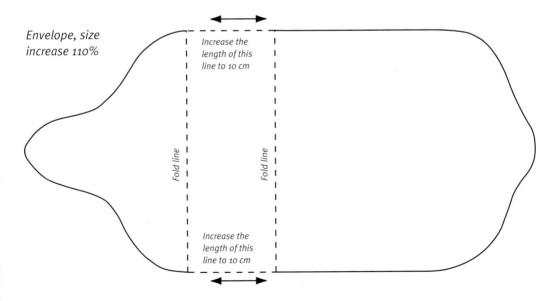

Envelope, size increase 110%

Increase the length of this line to 10 cm

Fold line

Fold line

Increase the length of this line to 10 cm

Lots of little animals

What you need
- ❏ *Card: white embossing paper, lavender blue (C150), lavender (P21) and violet (P20)*
- ❏ *Cutting sheet: Mini 3D AM 1002*
- ❏ *Embossing stencils: AE 1201, AE 1202 and AE 1205*

1. Seals

Cut a lavender blue rectangle (21 x 18 cm) and a lavender rectangle (18 x 9 cm).
Use stencil 1202 to emboss the diamond shapes on the lavender card. Use stencil 1202 to emboss 6.5 cm wide stripes on the left and right-hand sides of the card. Stick everything together and fold the card. To produce a sharp fold, score the card first by running a ball-point pen along a ruler. Use stencil 1205 to emboss the large diamonds on the white embossing paper and the lavender card. Cut them out and stick them on top of each other (see photograph). Use 3D glue to stick them on the left and right-hand sides of the card. Shape the pictures and use 3D glue to stick them on the card.

2. Rabbits

Fold a lavender card (23 x 11.5 cm) double with the fold at the top. Use stencil 1202 to emboss the diamond shapes at the top and the stripes at the bottom. Cut a strip (11.5 x 3 cm) from the lavender blue card and a strip (11.5 x 2.5 cm) from the white embossing paper. Emboss two lines on the white strip and stick everything together on the card. Shape the pictures and use 3D glue to stick them on the card. To create a nice effect, have one ear of the rabbits further forward than the other ear.

3. When the cat's away ...

Fold lavender card (26 x 13 cm) double with the fold at the top. Use stencil 1202 to emboss two diagonal lines on the card and the diamond shapes above the lines. Cut away the bottom part of the front flap. Cut a lavender blue card to the right size. Use stencil 1202 to emboss the stripes and stick the card behind the front flap. Use stencil 1205 to emboss shapes on violet card and stick them on white embossing paper (see Techniques). Stick the shapes on the card using 3D glue. Shape the pictures and use 3D glue to stick them on the card.

4. Cuddly bears

Fold a lavender blue card (21 x 14.8 cm) double with the fold on the left-hand side. Cut a strip from violet card (14.8 x 5.5 cm) and a strip from white embossing paper (14.8 x 4.9 cm). Use stencil 1202 to emboss stripes on the right-hand side of the card. Stick the strips of card on top of each other and then stick them on the card. Emboss the squares on a piece of lavender card. Cut them out and use 3D glue to stick them on the card. Shape the polar bears and use 3D glue to stick them on the card.

5. Meow

Fold a lavender blue card (22 x 11.5 cm) double with the fold at the top. Use stencil 1202 to emboss two straight lines and the diamond shapes above the lines. Cut the front flap off along the straight lines. Cut a lavender card to the right size. Use stencil 1202 to emboss the stripes on this card and stick the card behind the front flap. Use stencil 1205 to emboss the shapes on white card and stick them on violet card (see Techniques). Use 3D glue to stick them on the card. Shape the pictures and use 3D glue to stick them on the card.

6. Penguins

Fold a strip of lavender blue card (30 x 9.5 cm) 21.5 cm from the left-hand side. Use stencil 1201 to emboss two wavy lines and the stripes on the card. Cut the card off along the wavy lines. Cut a lavender card to the right size. Use stencil 1202 to emboss the diamond shapes on this card. Stick the card behind the front flap with the wavy lines. Use stencil 1205 to emboss the large diamonds on the white embossing paper and cut them out. Stick them on violet card and cut them out leaving a 2 mm wide border. Use 3D glue to stick the diamonds on the card. Shape the penguins and use 3D glue to stick them on the diamonds.

Spring

What you need
- ❏ Card: ivory (C111), bright yellow (C400) and mango (A575)
- ❏ Cutting sheets: Shake-it (IT 343 and IT 347)
- ❏ Embossing stencils: AE 1204 and AE 1205

1. White narcissus

Fold a piece of ivory card (26 x 13 cm) 8 cm from the left-hand side and 5 cm from the right-hand side. Use stencil 1204 to emboss the two wavy lines on each side. Use stencil 1204 to fill the left-hand side with embossed flowers and emboss two flowers on the right-hand side. Cut the card off along the wavy lines leaving a small border. Cut a piece of bright yellow card to the right size for the middle part of the card. Use stencil 1204 to emboss stripes on this card. Stick it inside the card. Use stencil 1205 to emboss the shapes on bright yellow card and stick them mango card (see Techniques). Make the narcissus 3D.

2. Everything in order

Fold a bright yellow card (21 x 20 cm) double with the fold at the top. Use stencil 1204 to emboss the wavy lines. Move the stencil to increase the length of the lines. Emboss the flowers above the lines. Cut the card off along the wavy lines leaving a border. Cut a piece of ivory card to the right size and use stencil 1204 to emboss stripes on it. Stick it behind the front flap. Use stencil 1205 to emboss four shapes and cut them out leaving a border. Use 3D glue to stick them on the card. Make the pictures 3D.

3. Envelope

Cut a piece of ivory card to the right size (see drawing on page 6) and fold it as indicated. Use stencil 1204 to emboss stripes on the parts which have been folded inwards. Cut a piece of bright yellow card to the right size (see drawing on page 7) and fold it as indicated. Use stencil 1204 to emboss the left-hand flap with flowers and emboss two flowers on the right-hand flap. Use stencil 1205 to emboss the shape and cut it out leaving a border. Use 3D glue to stick it on

Continued on page 15

Say it with flowers

1. Open squares

Fold a white card (26 x 13 cm) double with the fold on the left-hand side. Use a pencil to mark the inside of the card where the lines will be embossed and use stencil 1202 to emboss the lines. Emboss the diamond shapes in the bottom left-hand corner and the top right-hand corner. Use stencil 1205 to emboss the squares in the top left-hand corner and bottom right-hand corner. Cut out the inside of these squares. Cut a piece of apple green card to the right size and stick it behind the front flap. Cut the squares out slightly smaller to leave an apple green border. Cut a piece of wine red card to the right size and stick it against the inside of the card. Stick the flowers inside the card in the open squares and make them 3D.

2. Greetings

Fold an apple green card (21 x 19 cm) double with the fold at the top. Cut a 2 cm strip off of the bottom. Use stencil 1202 to emboss the diamond shapes on the front, leaving a piece on the left-hand side unembossed. Cut a piece of wine red card to the right size and stick it behind the front flap to create a border. Cut a piece of white card to the right size and use stencil 1202 to emboss the stripes at the bottom. Stick it behind the front flap. Use white and wine red card to make the large diamonds. Use more 3D glue for the right-hand diamond than for the left-hand diamond. Make the tulips 3D on the diamonds.

3. Label

Fold a wine red card (13 x 6.5 cm) double with the fold on the left-hand side. Use stencil 1202 to emboss the diamond shapes. Use stencil 1205 to emboss the square on white card and cut it out leaving a border. Use 3D glue to stick it on the card. Stick a flower on the shape and make it 3D. Use the hole punch to punch a hole in the card and thread a gold thread through the hole.

4. Get well soon

Fold an apple green card (21 x 20 cm) double with the fold on the left-hand side. Use stencil 1202 to emboss diamond shapes on the left-hand side and the stripes on the right-hand side. Emboss a straight line on both sides of a 2.5 cm wide strip of white card. Stick it on wine red card and cut it out leaving a border. Stick the strip on the card. Use stencil 1205 to emboss the large shapes: one on white card and one on apple green card. Cut them out leaving a border and stick them on card of the other colour. Also cut these out leaving a border and use 3D glue to stick them on the card. Stick the flowers on the shapes and make them 3D.

5. Tulip

Fold a green card (21 x 19 cm) double with the fold at the top. Use stencil 1202 to emboss the diamond shapes at the top and the stripes at the bottom of a piece of white card (18.5 x 10 cm). Stick this on the card. Emboss a line on both sides of a 2.5 cm wide strip of wine red card. Stick it on green card and cut it out leaving a 2 mm wide border. Stick this on the card. Make the shape as explained for card 4. Make the tulip 3D.

Continued from page 11 (Spring)

the left-hand flap. Make sure the right-hand flap can be stuck under the shape by not applying 3D glue under the right-hand side. Cut deep incisions in the crocus leaves. Shape them and make them 3D.

4. Get well soon

Fold a piece of bright yellow card (29.7 x 10 cm) 9.9 cm from both sides. Cut the right-hand side diagonally through the middle and use stencil 1204 to emboss stripes on this side of the card. Use stencil 1204 to emboss two wavy lines on the left-hand side of the card. Also emboss

flowers on this side of the card. Cut the card off along the wavy lines leaving a border. Cut a piece of ivory card to the right size and stick it inside the card. Use stencil 1205 to emboss the shape on ivory card and stick it on mango card (see Techniques). Finally, stick the narcissus on the shape and make it 3D.

5. Triptych

This card is made in almost the same way as card 1 of Hollyhocks and violets (see page 31). However, use ivory, bright yellow and mango card and stencils 1204 and 1205 for these cards.

Violets

1. 'How are you' label

Use stencil 1206 to emboss the tulip shape on purple card. Cut the shape out leaving a border and stick it on white card. Cut the white card to leave a border. Use the hole punch to punch a hole in the top left-hand corner and thread a gold thread through the hole. Stick a small violet on the card and make it 3D. Decorate the card with a sticker and a label.

2. 'Thank you' label

See the description given for card 1. Use lilac card instead of purple card.

3. Good luck

Fold a white card (29.7 x 8.5 cm) 7.4 cm from the left and right-hand sides. Use stencil 1203 to emboss the wavy lines. Use the same stencil to emboss the stripes, making sure the stripes do not run into the wavy lines. Cut the card off along lines leaving a border. Cut a lilac rectangle (14.7 x 11.5 cm). Emboss the lines at the top of the card as shown in the photograph. Use stencil 1203 to emboss the lilies on purple card and cut the card off along the lines leaving a border. Stick the card against the inside of the card. Use stencil 1206 to emboss the shapes on purple and lilac card. Cut them out leaving a border and stick them on card of the other colour. Also cut these out leaving a border. Use normal glue to stick the left-hand shape on the card and use 3D glue to stick the right-hand shape on the card. Make the violets 3D.

4. For no reason

Fold a white card (26 x 13 cm) double with the fold on the left-hand side. Cut a strip (26 x 10.5 cm) of lilac card and use stencil 1203 to emboss wavy lines on it. Use a pencil to mark on the back where you wish to emboss the wavy lines. Use stencil 1203 to emboss the stripes, making sure the stripes do not go all

the way through the wavy lines. Cut the card off along the wavy lines leaving a border. Emboss the lilies on white card and stick everything together. Use stencil 1205 to emboss the shapes on white card. Cut them out leaving a border and stick them on purple card. Cut them out leaving a border. Use normal glue to stick the right-hand shape on the card and then use 3D glue to stick the left-hand shape on the card. Make the violets 3D.

5. Good luck

Fold a white card (29.7 x 10.5 cm) double with the fold at the top. Use a pencil to mark the back of the card where you wish to emboss the wavy lines and use stencil 1202 to emboss the lines. Use stencil 1203 to emboss the lilies. Cut the card off along the wavy lines. Cut a piece of purple card to the right size. Use stencil 1203 to emboss the stripes and stick it behind the front flap. Emboss two tulip shapes on lilac card and cut them out with a 2 mm wide border. Use 3D glue to stick them on the card. Cut deep incisions in the crocus leaves. Shape them and stick them on the card using 3D glue. Make them 3D.

6. Greetings from ...

Fold a lilac card (21 x 18 cm) double with the fold on the left-hand side. Use stencil 1205 to emboss the four shapes on the card. Use stencil 1203 to emboss the lilies around the shapes. Cut the inside of the four shapes out leaving a border. Cut a piece of purple card to the right size and stick it behind the front flap. Cut the inside of the shapes out again leaving a border. Cut deep incisions in the leaves of the small violets. Shape them and use 3D glue to stick them in the openings. Make them 3D.

7. Get well soon

Fold a white card (21 x 20 cm) double with the fold at the top. Use stencil 1202 to emboss two wavy lines. Increase the length of the lines by moving the stencil. Use stencil 1203 to emboss the lilies. Cut the card off along the lines. Cut a piece of purple card to the right size and use stencil 1203 to emboss the stripes on it. Stick it behind the front flap. Use stencil 1205 to emboss the shapes on lilac card and stick them on purple card (see Techniques). Make the violets 3D.

Baby Boy

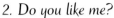

What you need

- Card: white (C335), ice blue (P42) and iris blue (P31)
- Cutting sheets: Babies 1 and 2 (AK 019, AK 020) and Mini 3D (AM 1003)
- Embossing stencils: AE 1201, AE 1204 and AE 1206
- Circle cutter
- Gold thread
- Hole punch

Shape the pictures using the shaping pen and use 3D glue to stick them on the card.

1. A cute little cat

Fold a white card (20 x 13.5 cm) double with the fold at the top. Use stencil 1201 to emboss the dots. Cut an iris blue circle (Ø 11 cm) and emboss the stripes on it. Stick the circle on the card which has been folded open and use the shaping pen to score the fold. Use stencil 1206 to emboss the shapes on iris blue card and cut them out roughly. Stick them on iris blue card and cut them out leaving a 2 mm wide border. Use 3D glue to stick them on the card.

2. Do you like me?

Fold an ice blue card (26 x 13 cm) double with the fold on the left-hand side. Use stencil 1201 to first emboss two wavy lines and then the dots. Cut the card off along the lines leaving a border. Cut an iris blue card to the right size and emboss the stripes on it. Stick it behind the front flap. Use stencil 1206 to emboss the shapes on white card and cut them out. Stick them on iris blue card and cut them out leaving a 2 mm wide border. Use 3D glue to stick them on the card.

3. A boy

Fold an ice blue card (20 x 15.5 cm) double with the fold on the left-hand side. Use stencil 1206 to emboss the two shapes and use stencil 1201 to emboss the dots. Cut the inside of the shapes out. Cut a piece of white card to the right size and stick it inside the card. Stick the pictures in the openings.

4. Peek-a-boo

Use an iris blue card (10 x 7 cm) for this label. Fold it double and use stencil 1201 to emboss some stripes at an angle. Stick the picture on white card and cut it out leaving a border.

Continued on page 23

Baby Girl

What you need
- ❑ Card: white (C335), blossom (P34), cerise (P33) and pink (P15)
- ❑ Cutting sheets: Babies 1 and 2 (AK 019, AK 020) and Mini 3D babies AM 1003
- ❑ Embossing stencils: AE 1204 and AE 1205
- ❑ Circle cutter
- ❑ Hole punch
- ❑ Organza ribbon

1. Lots of rabbits

Fold a blossom card (18 x 14 cm) double with the fold at the top. Use stencil 1204 to emboss the wavy lines and the flowers. Cut the card off along the lines leaving a border. Cut a piece of cerise card to the right size. Stick it behind the front flap and cut it off leaving a border. Cut a piece of white card to the right size. Use stencil 1204 to emboss the stripes and stick it behind the front flap. Shape the pictures and use 3D glue to stick them on the card. For a nice effect, have one ear facing more forwards than the other ear.

2. Baby with a cat

Fold a cerise card (26 x 13 cm) double with the fold at the top. Use stencil 1204 to emboss the wavy lines and then emboss the flowers. Cut the card off along the wavy lines leaving a border. Cut a piece of blossom card to the right size and use stencil 1204 to emboss stripes on it. Stick it behind the front flap. Use stencil 1205 to decorate the shape as described for card 3.

3. Round card with a stand

Cut a cerise circle (Ø 11.5 cm) and a blossom circle (Ø 11 cm). Use stencil 1204 to emboss two curved lines on the blossom card. Use the same stencil to emboss flowers above the lines and stripes below the lines. Stick this on the large circle. Use stencil 1205 to emboss the figure on white card and stick it on pink card (see Techniques). Shape the picture and use 3D glue to stick it on the card. Use the hole punch to punch two holes in the top left-hand corner of the card. Thread the ribbon through the holes and tie it in a bow. The pattern for the stand is shown on page 23.

4. Card with a dummy

Cut a cerise circle (Ø 14 cm) and a blossom circle (Ø 13 cm). Fold the circles double. Place one inside the other as shown in the photograph. Stick the backs of the cards together with the cerise card at the back and the blossom card at the front. Cut the cards straight at the bottom so that they can stand up. Use stencil 1204 to emboss flowers on the left-hand side and stripes on the right-hand side. Use stencil 1205 to make the square shape (see Techniques) and

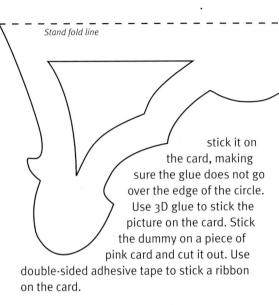

Stand fold line

Stand pattern (full size)

stick it on the card, making sure the glue does not go over the edge of the circle. Use 3D glue to stick the picture on the card. Stick the dummy on a piece of pink card and cut it out. Use double-sided adhesive tape to stick a ribbon on the card.

5. Do you like my hair?

Fold a blossom card (22 x 11 cm) double with the fold on the left-hand side. Use stencil 1204 to emboss the flowers. Make the shape as described for card 2, except use cerise card instead of pink card as the background. Use 3D glue to stick the shape and the picture on the card. Use the hole punch to punch two holes in the top left-hand corner of the card. Thread a ribbon the hole and tie it in a bow.

Baby boy continued from page 19

Use 3D glue to stick it on the label. Use a hole punch to punch a hole in the top left-hand corner and thread a gold thread through the hole.

5. A baby

Fold a white rectangle (29.7 x 10 cm) 9.9 cm from both sides. Cut the right-hand side diagonally through the middle. Use stencil 1204 to emboss the curved line on the left-hand side and then use stencil 1201 to emboss the dots. Cut the card off along the curved line. Cut a piece of ice blue card to the right size for the

middle section and emboss the stripes on it. Stick it inside the card.

6. Sleep tight

Fold an iris blue card (26 x 13 cm) double with the fold on the left-hand side. Cut a white card (12.5 x12.3 cm). Use stencil 1204 to emboss two curved lines and stencil 1201 to emboss the dots at the top and the stripes at the bottom. Cut the white card 2 mm above the curved lines in half and stick it on the card so that the iris blue can be seen in between. Use stencil 1206 to emboss two shapes. Cut them out and use 3D glue to stick them on the card.

Grape hyacinths

What you need
- ❏ *Card: ivory (C111) and lavender blue (C150)*
- ❏ *Cutting sheets: grape hyacinths, Shake-it 3D - Collage (IT 348)*
- ❏ *Embossing stencils: AE 1203, AE 1205 and AE 1206*
- ❏ *Parchment (Congratulations - blue) ITV 104*
- ❏ *Aslan*

1. Congratulations

Fold an ivory card (29.7 x 9.5 cm) 5.8 cm from the left-hand side and 9.8 cm from the left and right-hand sides. Use stencil 1203 to emboss lilies in the middle section of the card and then two curved lines and stripes on the side flaps. Cut the card off along the curved lines leaving a border. Cut two rectangles (9.5 x 6.5 cm) from blue card. Stick them behind the side flaps and cut them off leaving a 2 mm wide border. Use stencil 1206 to emboss the shapes in blue card. Cut these out leaving a border and use 3D glue to stick them on the card. Shape the pictures and use 3D glue to stick them on the card.

2. Blue shapes and grape hyacinths

Fold an ivory card (21 x 14.8 cm) double with the fold at the top. Use stencil 1203 to emboss the shell border twice and the lilies above them.

Cut the card off along the shell border leaving a border. Cut a piece of blue card to the right size. Emboss stripes on it and stick it behind the front flap. Use stencil 1206 to emboss two blue shapes and cut them out leaving a border. Use 3D glue to stick them on the card. Shape the grape hyacinths and use 3D glue to stick them on the blue shapes.

3. Triptych

Cut an ivory strip of card according to the diagram shown on page 26 to give you three squares (8 x 8 cm) with hinges between them. Use stencil 1203 to emboss lilies on the left and right-hand squares. Emboss some stripes on the left-hand side of the middle section. Use stencil 1205 to emboss the shapes on blue card. Cut them out leaving a border and use 3D glue to stick them on the card. The grape hyacinths on the middle square are stuck on with normal glue. Shape the other two pictures and use 3D glue to stick them on the left and right-hand squares.

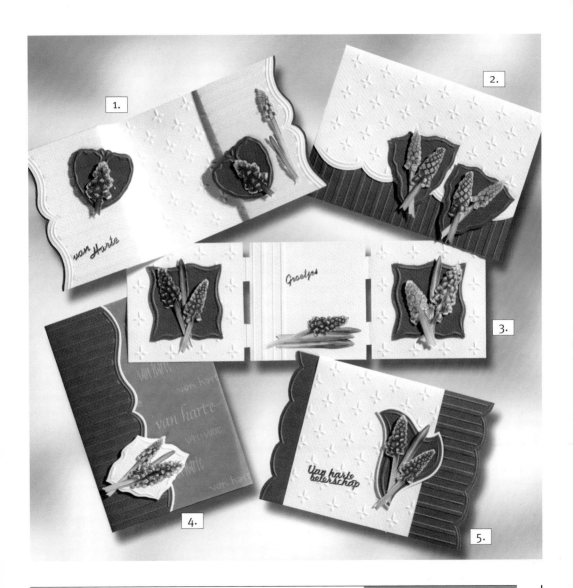

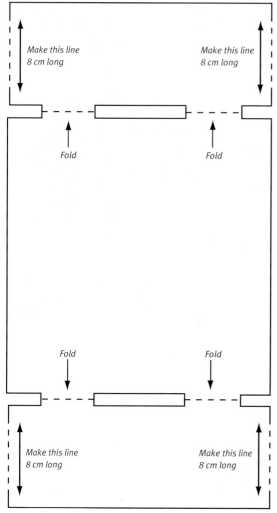

Make this line
8 cm long

Make this line
8 cm long

Fold

Fold

Fold

Fold

Make this line
8 cm long

Make this line
8 cm long

Triptych, size increase 110%

4. Congratulations (parchment)

Fold a blue rectangle (16 x 14.8 cm) 10.5 cm
from the left-hand side so that the narrow flap
is at the front. Use stencil 1203 to emboss the
curved line and then the stripes. Cut the card
off along the curved line leaving a border. Cut
a strip (14.8 x 5.5 cm) from ivory card. Stick it
behind the front flap and cut it off to leave a
2 mm wide border. Cut a piece of parchment
to the right size and use Aslan or a strip of
double-sided adhesive tape to stick it behind
the font on the card. Use stencil 1206 to
emboss the figure on ivory card and cut it out
leaving a border. Use 3D glue to stick it on the
card. Shape the grape hyacinths and use 3D
glue to stick them on the card.

5. Get well soon

Fold an ivory card (21 x 9 cm) double with the
fold at the top. Use stencil 1203 to emboss the
lilies. Take a piece of blue card (15 x 10.5 cm).
Emboss the shell border on the left-hand side
and emboss the shell border and some stripes
on the right-hand side. Stick it behind the front
of the ivory card. Use stencil 1206 to emboss
the shape in blue card. Cut it out leaving a
border. Stick it on ivory card and cut it out
leaving a 2 mm wide border. Use 3D glue to
stick it on the card. Shape the grape hyacinths
and use 3D glue to stick them on the shape.

Arums

1. Two white arums

Fold an ivory card (21 x 18 cm) double with the fold on the left-hand side. Use stencil 1202 to emboss the card. Emboss the straight line 4 cm from the fold, moving the stencil to increase the length of the line. Emboss the diamonds. Cut the card off along the line but keep a 2 cm wide strip of the ivory card. Cut a piece of yellow card to the right size and emboss stripes on it. Stick the strip of ivory card on the right-hand side of the yellow card and stick everything behind the front flap. Stick the flower on the card and make it 3D.

2. Congratulations

Fold an ivory card (26 x 13 cm) double with the fold at the top. Use stencil 1202 to emboss the diamonds. Cut a 3.3 cm wide strip from yellow card and use stencil 1202 to emboss straight lines on both sides of the strip. Stick the strip on apple green card and cut it out leaving a border. Stick everything on the card at an angle, making sure it does not stick over the edge of the card.

3. Congratulations

Fold a yellow card (21 x 18 cm) double with the fold on the left-hand side. Use stencil 1202 to emboss two wavy lines, moving the stencil to increase the length of the lines. Emboss the diamonds. Cut the card off along the lines leaving a border. Cut a piece of bright red card to the right size and stick it behind the front flap. Cut it off along the edge of the yellow card to leave a red border. Cut a piece of ivory card to the right size and emboss stripes on it. Stick it behind the front flap. Use stencil 1205 to emboss the shape. Cut it out leaving a border and stick it on bright red card. Cut this out to leave a border and use 3D glue to stick it on the card.

4. Envelope

Look at Spring, card 3, for a description of how to make this card. Use stencils 1202 and 1205 to make this envelope. Use yellow, ivory and apple green card.

5. Thanks!

Fold a yellow card (24 x 9 cm) 14 cm from the right-hand side. Use stencil 1202 to emboss the two curved lines and then the diamonds. Cut the card off along the lines leaving a border. Cut a piece of ivory card to the right size and emboss stripes on it. Stick it behind the front flap. Make the shape as described for card 3 and use 3D glue to stick everything on the card.

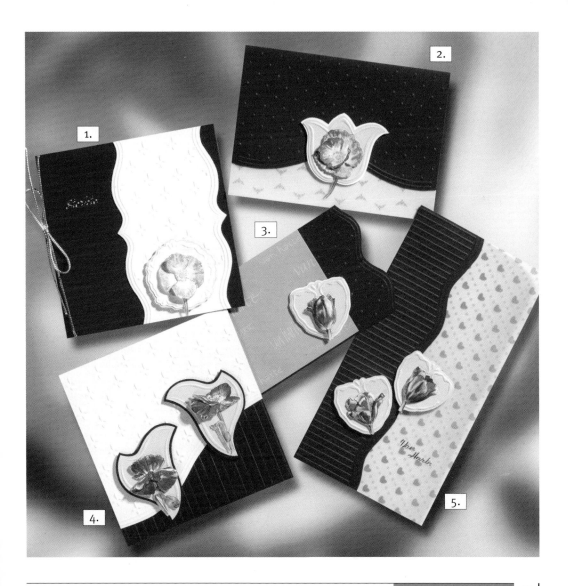

With love

What you need
- ❏ *Card: pink (A481), wine red (A519), white (C335)*
- ❏ *Shake-It cutting sheets: IT 332 and IT 328*
- ❏ *Embossing stencils: AE 1201, AE 1202, AE 1203, AE 1204, AE 1205 and AE 1206*
- ❏ *Gold thread*
- ❏ *Parchment: ITV 103, Congratulations and Erica's paper, Allure*

1. Get well soon

Fold a wine red card (26 x 13 cm) double with the fold on the left-hand side. Use stencil 1203 to emboss stripes up to 6 cm from the left-hand side. Use stencil 1203 to emboss wavy lines and then lilies on a piece of white card (13 x 9 cm). Cut the card off along the lines leaving a border and stick it on the card. Use stencil 1205 to emboss the shape on white and pink card. Stick the flower on the card and make it 3D. Tie a gold thread around the card.

2. Tulip or poppy

Fold a wine red card (21 x 15 cm) double with the fold at the top. Use stencil 1201 to emboss the two curved lines. Emboss dots above the lines. Cut the card off along the lines leaving a border. Stick pink card and the parchment behind the front flap. Use stencil 1206 to emboss the tulip shape on pink card. Cut it out and stick it on white card.

3. Congratulations (small card)

Fold a wine red card (17 x 14 cm) double with the fold at the top. Use stencil 1201 to emboss the two wavy lines. Cut the card off along the lines leaving a border. Fold parchment (16.9 x 9.5 cm) around the card and use double-sided adhesive tape to stick it to the back of the card. Use stencil 1201 to emboss the right-hand side with dots. Use stencil 1206 to emboss the heart shape on pink card and stick it on white card (see Techniques). Stick the picture on the card and make it 3D.

4. Two poppies

Fold a white card (26 x 13 cm) double with the fold at the top. Use stencil 1204 to emboss the curved lines. Emboss lilies above the lines. Cut the card off along the lines leaving a border. Use stencil 1203 to emboss stripes on wine red card and stick it behind the front flap. Use stencil 1206 to emboss two shapes on pink card. Cut them out and stick them on wine red card. Cut these out leaving a border and use 3D glue to stick them on the card. Make the poppy 3D.

5. Congratulations

Fold a wine red card (20 x 16 cm) 10.5 cm from the right-hand side. Use stencil 1202 to emboss the wavy lines. Move the stencil to increase the length of the lines. Cut the card off along the lines leaving a border. Use stencil 1201 to emboss the stripes. Make sure the stripes stop just before the wavy lines. Stick pink card and parchment behind the front flap. Use stencil 1206 to emboss the two shapes on pink card. Cut these out leaving a border and use 3D glue to stick them on the card. Make the tulips 3D on the shapes.

Hollyhocks and violets

What you need

- Card: white and pink embossing paper (K) and brick red (C505)
- Shake-it cutting sheets: violets, hollyhocks, IT 330, IT 354 and IT 364
- Embossing stencils: AE 1201 and AE 1206

Dark red violets (page 3)

Fold a pink card (26 x 13 cm) double with the fold at the top. Use stencil 1201 to emboss two curved lines. Emboss dots above the lines. Cut the card off along the lines leaving a border. Cut a piece of brick red card to the right size and use stencil 1201 to emboss stripes on it. Stick it behind the front flap. Use stencil 1206 to emboss the shapes on white card and stick them on brick red card (see Techniques). Make the violets 3D.

1. Triptych

Cut a strip of pink card to the right size (see diagram on page 26). Use stencil 1201 to emboss dots on the left and right-hand flaps. Emboss stripes on the middle section. Use stencil 1206 to emboss the tulip shape on white card. Cut it out leaving a border and stick it on brick red card. Cut it out leaving a border and use 3D glue to stick it on the right-hand flap. Cut deep incisions in the leaves of the flower, shape them and stick them on the card.

2. Waves

Fold a brick red card (21 x 14.8 cm) 6.5 cm from the left-hand side and 4 cm from the right-hand side. Use stencil 1201 to emboss two wavy lines on both sides. Next, emboss the dots. Cut the card off along the lines leaving a border. Cut a piece of pink card to the right size for the middle part of the card. Use stencil 1201 to emboss stripes on it, moving the stencil to increase the length of the stripes. Stick this inside the card. Use stencil 1206 to emboss the two shapes on white card and cut them out leaving a border. Stick them on the pink card and cut them out leaving a border. Use 3D glue to stick the two shapes on the card. Use more glue for the right-hand figure. Use 3D glue to stick the violets to the shapes and make them 3D.

3. Large violets

Fold a brick red card (26 x 13 cm) double with the fold at the top. Use stencil 1201 to emboss two wavy lines and then the dots. Cut the card off along the lines leaving a border. Cut a piece of white card to the right size and use stencil 1201 to emboss stripes on it.
Stick it behind the front flap. Use stencil 1205 to emboss the shapes on white card and stick them on pink card (see Techniques). Make the flowers 3D.

Many thanks to Avec B.V. in Waalwijk, the Netherlands, and Kars & Co B.V. in Ochten, the Netherlands, for providing the material.
The materials used can be ordered by shopkeepers from these companies.